Chapter 1: Understanding the Landscape of Home-Based Income

The Rise of Remote Work in 2024

In 2024, the rise of remote work has become a prominent trend in the modern workforce. With the advancements in technology and the increasing demand for flexibility, more and more people are choosing to work from home. This shift has opened up countless opportunities for individuals looking to earn an income without having to commute to a traditional office setting. The remote work landscape is evolving rapidly, and those who are able to adapt to this new way of working stand to benefit greatly.

One of the key factors driving the rise of remote work in 2024 is the increasing availability of remote job opportunities. Many companies are now offering remote positions as a way to attract top talent from around the world. This means that individuals no longer have to limit their job search to their local area, but can instead explore opportunities from companies based anywhere in the world. This has opened up a whole new world of possibilities for those looking to work from home and earn a steady income.

Another factor contributing to the rise of remote work is the flexibility it offers. Many people are drawn to the idea of being able to set their own hours and work from the comfort of their own home. This flexibility allows individuals to better balance their work and personal lives, leading to increased productivity and job satisfaction. With the ability to work remotely, individuals have the freedom to create a schedule that works best for them, allowing them to pursue other interests or responsibilities outside of work.

The rise of remote work in 2024 has also been fuelled by the increasing number of digital tools and platforms that make remote work more efficient and seamless. From video conferencing software to project management tools, there are countless resources available to help individuals collaborate and communicate effectively while working remotely. This has made it easier than ever for individuals to work from home and stay connected with their colleagues, regardless of physical distance.

Overall, the rise of remote work in 2024 presents a unique opportunity for individuals looking to earn an income from home. With the increasing availability of remote job opportunities, the flexibility of remote work, and the abundance of digital tools and platforms, there has never been a better time to explore the world of remote work. By embracing this trend and adapting to the changing landscape of the modern workforce, individuals can create a successful remote side hustle and earn $1000 a month from the comfort of their own home.

Benefits of Pursuing a Home-Based Income

Are you tired of the daily grind of the traditional 9-5 job? Do you dream of being your own boss and setting your own schedule? If so, pursuing a home-based income may be the perfect solution for you. In this subchapter, we will explore the benefits of working from home and how you can make $1000 a month in 2024 without ever having to leave the comfort of your own home.

One of the biggest benefits of pursuing a home-based income is the flexibility it offers. When you work from home, you have the freedom to set your own hours and work at your own pace. This means you can work early in the morning, late at night, or whenever it is most convenient for you. This flexibility allows you to better balance your work and personal life, leading to a happier and more fulfilling lifestyle.

Another benefit of working from home is the money you can save on commuting and other expenses. When you work from home, you no longer have to spend money on gas, public transportation, or eating out for lunch. This can add up to significant savings over time, allowing you to keep more of your hard-earned money in your pocket.

Working from home also allows you to avoid the stress and distractions of the traditional office environment. You can create a comfortable and productive workspace that is tailored to your needs, allowing you to focus on your work without the interruptions of coworkers or office politics. This can lead to increased productivity and job satisfaction, ultimately leading to a more successful and fulfilling career.

In addition to the financial and lifestyle benefits, pursuing a home-based income can also open up new opportunities for personal and professional growth. Working from home allows you to explore new skills and interests, take on different projects, and connect with a wider network of clients and collaborators. This can lead to new and exciting opportunities for career advancement and personal development, helping you to reach your full potential and achieve your goals.

Overall, pursuing a home-based income offers a wide range of benefits for adults looking to make $1000 a month from home in 2024. From increased flexibility and savings to improved work-life balance and personal growth, working from home can be a rewarding and fulfilling experience. So why wait? Start exploring your options for a home-based income today and take the first step towards building the career of your dreams.

Common Misconceptions about Working from Home

Working from home has become increasingly popular in recent years, with many people opting for the flexibility and convenience that comes with remote work. However, there are several common misconceptions about working from home that may prevent individuals from taking advantage of this opportunity. In this subchapter, we will debunk some of these myths and provide insights into how you can successfully earn $1000 a month from the comfort of your home in 2024.

One common misconception about working from home is that it is easy and requires little effort. While working from home does offer flexibility in terms of when and where you work, it still requires dedication, focus, and effort to be successful. In order to make $1000 a month from home, you will need to set goals, create a schedule, and stay disciplined in your work habits.

Another misconception about working from home is that it is only suitable for certain types of jobs or industries. In reality, there are a wide range of remote opportunities available in various fields, from customer service and data entry to freelance writing and graphic design. By exploring different options and leveraging your skills and experience, you can find a remote side hustle that aligns with your interests and goals.

Some people believe that working from home means being isolated and disconnected from colleagues and clients. However, with advancements in technology such as video conferencing and project management tools, it is easier than ever to stay connected and collaborate with others remotely. Building strong relationships with your virtual team members and clients is essential for success in a remote work environment.

It is also a common misconception that working from home is not as financially rewarding as traditional office-based jobs. In reality, there are many opportunities to earn a competitive income from home, whether through freelancing, online tutoring, virtual assistance, or e-commerce. By setting clear financial goals, managing your time effectively, and continuously improving your skills, you can increase your earning potential and achieve your target of making $1000 a month from home in 2024.

Chapter 2: Setting Up Your Home-Based Income Strategy

Assessing Your Skills and Interests

Assessing your skills and interests is a crucial first step in establishing a successful home-based income. Before diving into the world of remote side hustles, it's important to take stock of what you're good at and what you enjoy doing. By identifying your strengths and passions, you can tailor your income-generating activities to align with your personal goals and preferences.

Start by making a list of your skills, both technical and soft. Consider your professional experience, education, and any hobbies or interests that could translate into marketable skills. Are you a whiz at graphic design, a master of social media marketing, or a talented writer? Do you have a passion for photography, a knack for customer service, or a flair for organization? Identifying your unique talents will help you narrow down potential opportunities for generating income from home.

Next, think about what activities you enjoy doing in your spare time. Whether it's crafting, cooking, gardening, or playing music, there are countless ways to turn your hobbies into profitable side hustles. By focusing on activities that bring you joy, you'll be more motivated to put in the time and effort required to build a successful home-based income. Consider how you can leverage your interests to create products or services that resonate with potential customers in your niche.

Once you've identified your skills and interests, it's time to evaluate the market demand for your offerings. Research your target audience, competition, and potential income streams to determine the viability of your home-based business idea. Are there existing platforms or marketplaces where you can sell your products or services? What pricing strategies will allow you to remain competitive while still earning a sustainable income? By conducting thorough market research, you can ensure that your home-based income venture is both profitable and fulfilling.

In conclusion, assessing your skills and interests is a critical step in launching a successful home-based income. By identifying your unique strengths and passions, you can tailor your side hustle to align with your personal goals and preferences. Whether you're leveraging your professional experience, hobbies, or talents, taking the time to evaluate your market potential will set you up for success in the world of remote side hustles. With the right combination of skills, interests, and market research, you can make $1000 a month from home in 2024.

Researching Profitable Home-Based Income Opportunities

Researching profitable home-based income opportunities is a crucial step in achieving success in the world of remote side hustles. With the rise of technology and the increasing popularity of working from home, there are more opportunities than ever to make a substantial income without leaving the comfort of your own home. In this subchapter, we will explore the different ways you can research and find profitable home-based income opportunities that align with your skills and interests.

One of the first steps in researching profitable home-based income opportunities is to assess your skills and interests. Take some time to reflect on what you excel at and what you enjoy doing. This will help you narrow down your search and focus on opportunities that you are passionate about. Whether you have a background in writing, graphic design, programming, or customer service, there are countless ways to monetize your skills from home.

Once you have identified your skills and interests, the next step is to research different home-based income opportunities that align with them. Use online resources such as job boards, freelance websites, and social media platforms to explore different opportunities in your niche. Reach out to other remote workers in your field for advice and networking opportunities. The key is to gather as much information as possible to make an informed decision about which opportunities to pursue.

In addition to researching specific job opportunities, it is also important to research the market demand for your skills. Look for trends in your industry and identify areas of high demand where you can offer your services. Conduct market research to understand the needs of potential clients and tailor your services to meet those needs. By staying informed about market trends, you can position yourself as a valuable asset in the home-based income market.

Finally, don't be afraid to experiment and try out different income opportunities to see what works best for you. The beauty of working from home is the flexibility to try new things and pivot when necessary. Keep track of your income and expenses to determine which opportunities are most profitable for you. By staying open-minded and willing to adapt, you can maximize your earning potential and achieve success in the world of home-based income.

Creating a Realistic Monthly Income Goal

Creating a realistic monthly income goal is an essential step in achieving financial success through a home-based side hustle. Setting a specific target amount, such as $1000 a month, gives you a clear objective to work towards and helps you stay motivated and focused on your income-generating activities.

To determine your monthly income goal, start by evaluating your current financial situation and expenses. Calculate your monthly bills, including rent or mortgage, utilities, groceries, transportation, and any other necessary expenses. Once you have a clear understanding of your monthly spending, you can determine how much extra income you need to cover your expenses and reach your financial goals.

When setting your monthly income goal, it's important to be realistic and consider factors such as the amount of time you can dedicate to your side hustle, your skills and experience, and the market demand for your services or products. Setting an overly ambitious goal can lead to frustration and burnout, while setting a goal that is too low may not provide enough motivation to drive your success.

To increase your chances of reaching your monthly income goal, break it down into smaller, achievable milestones. For example, if your goal is to make $1000 a month, aim to earn $250 a week or $50 a day. Setting smaller targets allows you to track your progress more easily and make adjustments to your strategy if needed.

In conclusion, creating a realistic monthly income goal is a crucial step in achieving success with a home-based side hustle. By evaluating your current financial situation, setting a specific target amount, and breaking it down into smaller milestones, you can stay focused, motivated, and on track to reach your income goals. With dedication, hard work, and a strategic plan, you can make $1000 a month from home in 2024.

Chapter 3: Implementing Profitable Home-Based Income Strategies

Freelancing in High-Demand Industries

In today's digital age, freelancing has become a popular option for individuals looking to supplement their income or make a full-time living. One of the key advantages of freelancing is the ability to work from home, allowing individuals to create their own schedules and work on projects that interest them. In this subchapter, we will explore freelancing in high-demand industries and how you can leverage your skills to make $1000 a month in 2024.

One of the most lucrative industries for freelancers is technology. With the increasing demand for software development, web design, and digital marketing services, there is no shortage of opportunities for skilled individuals in the tech industry. Whether you are a programmer, graphic designer, or social media expert, there are plenty of freelance gigs available that can help you reach your income goals.

Another high-demand industry for freelancers is healthcare. With the rise of telemedicine and remote patient monitoring, there is a growing need for healthcare professionals to provide their services online. If you are a nurse, therapist, or medical transcriptionist, you can easily find freelance work in the healthcare industry that can help you earn $1000 a month from the comfort of your own home.

The creative industry is also a great option for freelancers looking to make a living from home. Whether you are a writer, photographer, or video editor, there are plenty of opportunities to showcase your talents and attract clients who are willing to pay for your services. By leveraging your creative skills and building a strong portfolio, you can easily secure freelance gigs that can help you achieve your income goals.

In addition to technology, healthcare, and creative industries, there are plenty of other high-demand industries that offer lucrative opportunities for freelancers. From consulting and coaching to e-commerce and virtual assistance, there are endless possibilities for individuals looking to make $1000 a month from home in 2024. By identifying your skills and interests, you can easily find freelance gigs that align with your goals and help you achieve financial success in the remote side hustle.

Starting a Profitable Online Business

In this subchapter, we will delve into the world of starting a profitable online business from the comfort of your own home. With the rise of technology and the internet, it has never been easier to create a successful online business that can generate a steady income. Whether you are looking to supplement your current income or make a full-time living, the opportunities are endless in the digital age.

The first step in starting a profitable online business is to identify a niche that interests you and has the potential to generate income. This could be anything from selling handmade crafts on Etsy to offering consulting services in your area of expertise. By choosing a niche that you are passionate about, you are more likely to stay motivated and dedicated to growing your business.

Once you have identified your niche, it is important to research your target market and competition. Understanding who your potential customers are and what sets you apart from your competitors will help you create a unique selling proposition that attracts customers to your business. By conducting market research and analysing your competition, you can identify gaps in the market and tailor your products or services to meet the needs of your target audience.

Next, you will need to establish an online presence for your business. This includes creating a professional website, setting up social media accounts, and utilizing online marketing strategies to drive traffic to your site. By creating a strong online presence, you can reach a wider audience and attract potential customers from around the world.

Finally, to ensure the success of your online business, it is important to continuously monitor and adjust your strategies based on performance data. By tracking key metrics such as website traffic, conversion rates, and customer feedback, you can identify areas for improvement and make necessary adjustments to optimize your business for profitability. With dedication, perseverance, and a strategic approach, you can build a profitable online business that generates a steady income from the comfort of your own home.

Monetizing Your Hobbies and Passions

Monetizing your hobbies and passions can be a rewarding way to earn extra income from the comfort of your own home. Whether you love crafting, gardening, cooking, or photography, there are numerous ways to turn your interests into a profitable side hustle. By leveraging your skills and creativity, you can generate a steady stream of income while doing what you love.

One way to monetize your hobbies is by selling your creations online. Platforms like Etsy, eBay, and Amazon Handmade allow you to reach a global audience and sell your handmade goods to customers around the world. Whether you specialize in handmade jewellery, knitted scarves, or custom artwork, there is a market for your unique creations. By setting up an online store and promoting your products through social media and online marketing, you can turn your hobby into a profitable business.

Another way to monetize your hobbies is by offering your services as a freelancer or consultant. If you have a passion for writing, graphic design, web development, or social media marketing, there are countless opportunities to work as a freelance professional from home. Websites like Upwork, Fiverr, and Freelancer connect freelancers with clients in need of their services, allowing you to showcase your skills and expertise to potential clients. By building a strong portfolio and reputation as a freelancer, you can attract high-paying clients and generate a steady income from your passion.

In addition to selling products and services, you can also monetize your hobbies by teaching others. Whether you are an expert in knitting, cooking, gardening, or photography, there are people willing to pay for your knowledge and expertise. By offering online courses, workshops, or one-on-one coaching sessions, you can share your skills with others and earn money in the process. Platforms like Teachable, Udemy, and Skill share make it easy to create and sell online courses, allowing you to reach a global audience and generate passive income from your passion.

Overall, monetizing your hobbies and passions is a great way to earn extra income and turn your interests into a profitable side hustle. By leveraging your skills, creativity, and expertise, you can create a successful home-based business that allows you to do what you love while making money. Whether you choose to sell products, offer services as a freelancer, or teach others, there are endless opportunities to monetize your hobbies and generate a steady stream of income from home. With dedication, hard work, and a passion for your craft, you can achieve financial success and build a fulfilling career doing what you love.

Chapter 4: Maximizing Your Earning Potential from Home

Time Management Techniques for Home-Based Income

Time management is crucial for anyone looking to make a sustainable income from home. With the rise of remote side hustles in 2024, it has become more important than ever to effectively manage your time to maximize your earning potential. In this subchapter, we will discuss some key time management techniques that can help you achieve your goal of making $1000 a month from the comfort of your own home.

One of the most effective time management techniques for home-based income is to create a daily schedule. By setting aside specific blocks of time for work, breaks, and personal activities, you can ensure that you stay focused and productive throughout the day. This will help you avoid distractions and procrastination, allowing you to make the most of your time and increase your overall productivity.

Another important time management technique is to prioritize your tasks. Make a list of all the tasks you need to complete each day, and then prioritize them based on their importance and deadline. By focusing on the most important tasks first, you can ensure that you are making progress towards your income goals every day. This will also help you avoid feeling overwhelmed by a long list of tasks, as you can break them down into manageable chunks and tackle them one at a time.

Setting boundaries is another key time management technique for home-based income. It can be easy to let work bleed into your personal time when you are working from home, but it is important to set boundaries and stick to them. This means establishing a designated workspace, setting specific work hours, and avoiding distractions during those times. By creating a clear divide between work and personal time, you can ensure that you are able to focus on your income-generating activities without getting burned out.

Finally, learning to delegate tasks and outsource work can be a valuable time management technique for home-based income. If you find yourself overwhelmed with tasks or struggling to keep up with your workload, consider hiring freelancers or virtual assistants to help you. By outsourcing tasks that are outside your expertise or that take up too much of your time, you can free up more time to focus on income-generating activities and grow your home-based income even further. By implementing these time management techniques, you can increase your productivity, stay focused on your goals, and ultimately achieve success in your remote side hustle in 2024.

Marketing Your Home-Based Income Services

Marketing your home-based income services is a crucial step in growing your business and reaching your financial goals. In today's digital age, there are countless ways to promote your services and attract clients from the comfort of your own home. By utilizing a combination of online and offline marketing strategies, you can effectively showcase your skills and expertise to potential customers.

One of the most effective ways to market your home-based income services is through social media. Platforms like Facebook, Instagram, and LinkedIn offer a powerful way to connect with potential clients and showcase your work. By creating engaging posts, sharing client testimonials, and offering special promotions, you can attract a steady stream of new customers to your business.

In addition to social media, creating a professional website is essential for marketing your home-based income services. Your website should include a portfolio of your work, a list of services you offer, and contact information for potential clients to reach out to you. By investing in a well-designed website, you can establish credibility and attract clients who are searching for your specific skill set.

Networking is another important marketing strategy for promoting your home-based income services. By attending industry events, joining online forums, and connecting with other professionals in your field, you can build relationships and generate referrals for your business. Networking is a valuable way to expand your client base and establish yourself as an expert in your niche.

Lastly, don't underestimate the power of word-of-mouth marketing. Encourage satisfied clients to refer their friends and family to your services, and offer incentives for referrals. By providing exceptional service and delivering results, you can build a loyal customer base that will help promote your home-based income services through positive reviews and recommendations. Marketing your home-based income services is all about showcasing your skills, connecting with potential clients, and building relationships that will help your business thrive. By leveraging the power of social media, creating a professional website, networking with industry professionals, and encouraging word-of-mouth referrals, you can effectively market your services and achieve your financial goals from the comfort of your own home.

Building a Strong Online Presence to Attract Clients

Building a strong online presence is crucial for attracting clients to your home-based business. In today's digital age, having a solid online presence can make all the difference in reaching your target audience and growing your client base. By following a few key strategies, you can effectively establish and maintain a strong online presence that will help you attract clients and increase your income.

First and foremost, it's important to have a professional website for your home-based business. Your website is often the first impression potential clients will have of your business, so it's essential that it is well-designed, easy to navigate, and provides all the necessary information about your products or services. Be sure to include a clear call-to-action on your website, such as a contact form or button for clients to easily get in touch with you.

In addition to having a professional website, it's also important to maintain a strong presence on social media platforms. Social media is a powerful tool for connecting with clients, sharing information about your business, and building relationships with your target audience. Choose the platforms that are most relevant to your niche and target audience, and regularly post engaging content that showcases your expertise and offerings.

Another key aspect of building a strong online presence is utilizing search engine optimization (SEO) techniques to improve your website's visibility in search engine results. By optimizing your website for relevant keywords and creating high-quality, valuable content, you can increase your chances of appearing at the top of search results when potential clients are looking for products or services like yours.

Lastly, don't underestimate the power of online networking and collaborations in building your online presence. Connect with other businesses, influencers, and industry professionals in your niche to expand your reach and attract new clients. By working together and cross-promoting each other's businesses, you can tap into new audiences and opportunities for growth. Building a strong online presence takes time and effort, but by following these strategies and staying consistent in your efforts, you can effectively attract clients to your home-based business and increase your income.

Chapter 5: Overcoming Challenges and Roadblocks in Home-Based Income

Dealing with Isolation and Loneliness

Dealing with isolation and loneliness can be a common challenge for adults who are pursuing a remote side hustle from home. Working from home can often mean spending long hours alone, without the social interaction that comes with a traditional office environment. This can lead to feelings of isolation and loneliness, which can have a negative impact on mental health and overall well-being.

One way to combat feelings of isolation and loneliness when working from home is to make an effort to stay connected with others. This can be done through regular video calls with friends and family, joining online communities or forums related to your side hustle, or even reaching out to other remote workers for support and camaraderie. By maintaining connections with others, you can help alleviate feelings of loneliness and isolation.

Another way to combat isolation and loneliness when working from home is to establish a routine that includes regular breaks and time for social interaction. Taking breaks to go for a walk, call a friend, or participate in a virtual exercise class can help break up the monotony of working alone and provide much-needed social interaction. Additionally, scheduling regular social activities outside of work, such as joining a club or hobby group, can help you stay connected with others and combat feelings of isolation.

It's also important to prioritize self-care when dealing with isolation and loneliness while working from home. This can include taking time for yourself to relax and unwind, practicing mindfulness or meditation, getting regular exercise, and making sure to eat healthily. By taking care of your physical and mental well-being, you can better cope with feelings of isolation and loneliness and maintain a healthy work-life balance.

Lastly, if feelings of isolation and loneliness persist, it may be helpful to seek support from a mental health professional. Talking to a therapist or counsellor can provide valuable insights and strategies for coping with feelings of isolation and loneliness, and help you develop a plan for maintaining your mental health while working from home. Remember, it's important to prioritize your well-being and seek help when needed to ensure a successful and fulfilling remote side hustle experience.

Managing Work-Life Balance while Working from Home

Managing work-life balance while working from home can be a challenge for many adults. With the rise of remote side hustles in 2024, it is important to find ways to balance work responsibilities with personal life to avoid burnout and maintain overall well-being. This subchapter will explore strategies and tips on how to effectively manage work-life balance while working from home.

One key tip for managing work-life balance while working from home is to establish a routine. Setting specific work hours and sticking to them can help create boundaries between work and personal time. This can help prevent work from spilling over into personal life and vice versa, allowing for a healthier balance between the two.

Another important aspect of managing work-life balance while working from home is to create a designated workspace. Having a dedicated area for work can help signal to your brain that it is time to focus and be productive. This can help increase efficiency during work hours and allow for better separation between work and personal life when work is done.

Additionally, taking breaks throughout the day is crucial for maintaining work-life balance while working from home. It is important to step away from work periodically to rest and recharge, whether it is going for a walk, doing a quick workout, or simply taking a few minutes to relax. This can help prevent burnout and improve overall productivity in the long run.

Lastly, communicating boundaries with family members or roommates is essential for managing work-life balance while working from home. Letting others know when you are working and when you are available for personal time can help prevent interruptions and allow for a more harmonious balance between work and personal life. By implementing these strategies and tips, adults can effectively manage work-life balance while working from home and achieve success in their remote side hustle endeavours in 2024.

Handling Rejection and Setbacks in Your Home-Based Income Journey

Rejection and setbacks are inevitable in any journey towards building a home-based income. As an adult looking to make $1000 a month from home in 2024, it is important to understand that not every opportunity will pan out as expected. However, it is crucial to have the resilience and determination to push through these challenges and continue working towards your financial goals.

One of the key ways to handle rejection and setbacks in your home-based income journey is to stay positive and maintain a growth mindset. Understand that rejection is not a reflection of your worth or abilities, but rather a learning experience that can help you improve and grow. Use setbacks as opportunities to reassess your strategies, learn from your mistakes, and come back stronger than before.

Another important aspect of handling rejection and setbacks is to seek feedback and guidance from others. Don't be afraid to reach out to mentors, peers, or experts in your field for advice and support. Sometimes an outside perspective can help you see things from a different angle and provide valuable insights on how to overcome challenges and move forward.

It is also essential to stay focused on your long-term goals and not let rejection or setbacks deter you from your path. Remember why you started your home-based income journey in the first place and keep that vision in mind as you navigate through obstacles. Stay committed to your goals and continue taking consistent action towards achieving them, no matter how many setbacks you encounter along the way.

In conclusion, handling rejection and setbacks in your home-based income journey requires resilience, positivity, and a growth mindset. By staying focused on your goals, seeking feedback and support from others, and using setbacks as learning opportunities, you can overcome challenges and ultimately achieve success in making $1000 a month from home in 2024. Remember that setbacks are just temporary obstacles on the road to success, and with determination and perseverance, you can overcome them and reach your financial goals.

Chapter 6: Scaling Your Home-Based Income to Reach $1000 a Month

Setting SMART Goals for Increasing Your Income

When it comes to increasing your income through a side hustle, setting SMART goals is essential for success. SMART goals are Specific, Measurable, Achievable, Relevant, and Time-bound. By following these principles, you can create a clear roadmap to reaching your financial goals. In this subchapter, we will delve into how to set SMART goals specifically tailored to increasing your income from home in 2024.

First and foremost, your goals should be Specific. Instead of setting a vague goal like "make more money," be specific about how much you want to increase your income by. For example, you could set a goal to increase your monthly income by $500 through your remote side hustle. This specificity will give you a clear target to work towards.

Next, your goals should be Measurable. This means that you should be able to track your progress towards achieving your goal. Using the example above, you could track your income each month to see if you are on target to reach your $500 goal. Measuring your progress will help keep you motivated and focused on your ultimate objective.

Achievability is another key component of setting SMART goals. It's important to set goals that are within reach and realistic for your current situation. If your side hustle is still in its early stages, setting a goal to increase your income by $2000 a month may not be achievable right away. Start with smaller, more attainable goals and gradually increase them as your business grows.

Relevance is also crucial when setting goals for increasing your income. Your goals should be directly related to your side hustle and aligned with your overall financial objectives. For example, if your ultimate goal is to quit your day job and work from home full-time, your SMART goals should be focused on increasing your income to make that transition possible.

Finally, your goals should be Time-bound. Setting a deadline for achieving your income goals will help keep you accountable and motivated. By giving yourself a specific timeframe, such as increasing your income by $500 a month within the next six months, you are more likely to stay focused and take consistent action towards reaching your goal. By setting SMART goals for increasing your income from home in 2024, you can create a clear path to financial success and achieve the ultimate goal of making $1000 a month through your remote side hustle.

Diversifying Your Income Streams

Diversifying your income streams is a crucial step in securing financial stability and independence. In today's rapidly changing economy, relying on a single source of income is no longer a viable option. By diversifying your income streams, you can protect yourself against unexpected financial setbacks and increase your overall earning potential.

One way to diversify your income streams is to explore different remote side hustles. In 2024, the gig economy is booming, and there are countless opportunities to make money from the comfort of your own home. Whether you have a specific skill or talent to offer, or you're simply looking to try something new, there are plenty of remote side hustle options available to suit your interests and schedule.

One popular remote side hustle option is freelancing. Freelancing allows you to work on a project-by-project basis, giving you the flexibility to choose your own hours and workload. Whether you're a writer, graphic designer, web developer, or social media manager, there are plenty of freelancing opportunities available online. By taking on multiple freelancing projects, you can quickly build up a steady stream of income.

Another way to diversify your income streams is to explore passive income opportunities. Passive income involves earning money without actively working for it, allowing you to generate income while you sleep. Some popular passive income streams include affiliate marketing, selling digital products, and investing in real estate or stocks. By incorporating passive income streams into your overall income strategy, you can create a more stable and secure financial future for yourself.

In conclusion, diversifying your income streams is a smart financial move that can help you achieve your financial goals and build wealth over time. By exploring different remote side hustle opportunities, such as freelancing and passive income streams, you can increase your earning potential and create a more secure financial future for yourself. Take the time to research and explore different income opportunities that align with your skills and interests, and start building a diversified income portfolio today.

Investing in Your Skills and Education to Boost Your Earning Potential

Investing in your skills and education is essential if you want to boost your earning potential in the remote side hustle industry. In today's competitive job market, having specialized skills and qualifications can set you apart from the competition and help you command a higher salary. By continuously improving your skills and knowledge, you can increase your value to employers and clients, ultimately leading to higher earning potential.

One way to invest in your skills and education is to take online courses or workshops related to your field of interest. There are countless platforms such as Coursera, Udemy, and LinkedIn Learning that offer a wide range of courses on topics such as digital marketing, graphic design, coding, and more. By investing in these courses, you can acquire new skills and stay up-to-date with the latest trends and technologies in your industry.

Another way to boost your earning potential is to pursue certifications or advanced degrees in your field. Many employers and clients value professionals who have obtained certifications or advanced degrees, as it demonstrates a commitment to continuous learning and professional development. By investing in further education, you can expand your knowledge base, enhance your skills, and increase your earning potential in the remote side hustle industry.

Networking is also an important aspect of investing in your skills and education. By connecting with other professionals in your industry, attending networking events, and joining professional organizations, you can gain valuable insights, learn from others, and potentially discover new opportunities for growth and advancement. Building a strong network can open doors to new clients, partnerships, and collaborations that can help you boost your earning potential in the remote side hustle industry.

In conclusion, investing in your skills and education is crucial if you want to succeed in the remote side hustle industry and boost your earning potential. By taking online courses, pursuing certifications, and networking with other professionals, you can enhance your skills, expand your knowledge base, and position yourself for success in the competitive job market.
Remember, continuous learning and professional development are key to thriving in today's rapidly changing economy.

Chapter 7: Staying Motivated and Consistent in Your Home-Based Income Endeavours

Creating a Sustainable Routine for Productivity

Creating a sustainable routine for productivity is crucial when it comes to building a successful home-based income. As adults looking to make $1000 a month from home in 2024, it's essential to establish a routine that allows you to effectively manage your time and resources. By following these simple steps, you can maximize your productivity and increase your chances of reaching your financial goals.

First and foremost, it's important to set specific and achievable goals for your home-based income venture. Whether you're looking to make $1000 a month or more, having a clear target in mind will help you stay focused and motivated. Break down your goals into smaller tasks and create a timeline for accomplishing them. This will help you stay on track and measure your progress along the way.

Next, establish a daily routine that works for you. Consider your most productive hours and plan your work schedule around them. Allocate time for tasks such as research, marketing, and client communication, and make sure to include breaks to avoid burnout. By creating a consistent routine, you can train your mind to be more efficient and productive during work hours.

Incorporate self-care activities into your daily routine to maintain a healthy work-life balance. Exercise, meditation, and proper nutrition can help boost your energy levels and improve your overall well-being. Taking care of yourself is essential for sustaining productivity in the long run, so make sure to prioritize self-care alongside your work responsibilities.

Lastly, stay organized and prioritize tasks based on their importance and deadlines. Use tools such as calendars, to-do lists, and project management software to keep track of your tasks and stay on top of your workload. By staying organized, you can avoid feeling overwhelmed and ensure that you're making progress towards your income goals consistently.

By creating a sustainable routine for productivity, you can increase your chances of success in your home-based income venture. Remember to set specific goals, establish a daily routine, prioritize self-care, and stay organized to maximize your productivity and achieve your financial objectives. With dedication and perseverance, you can make $1000 a month from home in 2024 and beyond.

Celebrating Small Wins and Milestones

Celebrating Small Wins and Milestones is an essential part of the journey to making $1000 a month from home in 2024. It is important to recognize and appreciate the progress you have made, no matter how small it may seem. By acknowledging your achievements, you can stay motivated and focused on reaching your ultimate goal of financial success.

One way to celebrate small wins and milestones is to set specific, achievable goals for yourself. Whether it's reaching a certain income milestone or completing a certain number of projects, having clear objectives can help you stay on track and measure your progress. When you reach these goals, take the time to celebrate and reward yourself for your hard work and dedication.

Another way to celebrate small wins and milestones is to share your achievements with others. Whether it's with friends, family, or your online community, sharing your successes can help keep you accountable and motivated. Plus, receiving positive feedback and encouragement from others can boost your confidence and drive to continue working towards your financial goals.

It's also important to acknowledge the effort and dedication it takes to achieve small wins and milestones. Making $1000 a month from home in 2024 is no easy feat, and every step forward is a testament to your hard work and perseverance. By recognizing and appreciating the work you put in, you can build confidence in your abilities and stay motivated to keep pushing forward.

In conclusion, celebrating small wins and milestones is a crucial aspect of achieving success in your home-based income journey. By setting goals, sharing your achievements, and acknowledging your efforts, you can stay motivated and focused on reaching your financial goals. So, take the time to celebrate your successes, no matter how small they may seem, and keep pushing towards making $1000 a month from home in 2024.

Connecting with Like-Minded Individuals for Support and Accountability

In the journey towards building a successful home-based income, connecting with like-minded individuals for support and accountability can make a significant difference in your progress. Whether you are starting a remote side hustle or looking to increase your monthly earnings to $1000 in 2024, having a support system can provide motivation, inspiration, and guidance along the way. By surrounding yourself with individuals who share similar goals and challenges, you can create a network of accountability that keeps you on track and motivated to achieve your financial targets.

One of the most effective ways to connect with like-minded individuals for support and accountability is through online communities and forums dedicated to remote side hustles and home-based income. These platforms provide a space for individuals to share their experiences, ask questions, and offer advice to one another. By actively participating in these communities, you can build relationships with others who are on a similar journey and gain valuable insights and feedback on your own endeavours. Additionally, these communities can serve as a source of motivation and encouragement during times of doubt or difficulty.

Another way to connect with like-minded individuals for support and accountability is to join or create a mastermind group focused on home-based income. A mastermind group is a small, intimate gathering of individuals with similar goals who meet regularly to discuss their progress, set goals, and hold each other accountable. By participating in a mastermind group, you can benefit from the collective wisdom, experience, and support of your peers, helping you stay focused, motivated, and on track towards achieving your financial targets.

Attending networking events, workshops, and conferences related to remote side hustles and home-based income is another valuable way to connect with like-minded individuals for support and accountability. These events provide an opportunity to meet and interact with others who share your interests and goals, as well as learn from experts in the field. By networking with others in person, you can build meaningful relationships, exchange ideas, and gain valuable insights and advice that can help you on your path to making $1000 a month from home in 2024.

Overall, connecting with like-minded individuals for support and accountability is essential for anyone looking to build a successful home-based income. By surrounding yourself with individuals who share similar goals and challenges, you can create a network of accountability that keeps you motivated, inspired, and on track towards achieving your financial targets. Whether through online communities, mastermind groups, or networking events, finding and connecting with others who are on a similar journey can provide the support and encouragement you need to succeed in your remote side hustle and reach your financial goals.

Chapter 8: The Future of Home-Based Income: Trends and Opportunities in 2024

Emerging Technologies Shaping the Home-Based Income Landscape

The landscape of home-based income opportunities is rapidly evolving thanks to emerging technologies that are reshaping the way we work. In this subchapter, we will explore some of the key technologies that are revolutionizing the home-based income landscape and creating new opportunities for individuals looking to make $1000 a month from the comfort of their own homes.

One of the most significant technologies shaping the home-based income landscape is artificial intelligence (AI). AI is being used to automate tasks that were previously time-consuming and labour-intensive, allowing individuals to focus on more high-value activities. For example, AI-powered chatbots can handle customer service inquiries, freeing up time for individuals to work on other income-generating projects.

Another technology that is having a major impact on home-based income opportunities is blockchain. Blockchain technology is revolutionizing the way transactions are conducted online, making it easier and more secure for individuals to buy and sell goods and services. This technology is opening up new avenues for individuals to start online businesses and generate income from anywhere in the world.

Virtual reality (VR) and augmented reality (AR) are also playing a role in shaping the home-based income landscape. These technologies are enabling individuals to create immersive online experiences, such as virtual tours of real estate properties or interactive training programs. This opens up new opportunities for individuals to monetize their expertise and create unique income streams.

The rise of the gig economy is another trend that is impacting the home-based income landscape. Platforms like TaskRabbit, Upwork, and Fiverr are connecting individuals with freelance work opportunities, allowing them to earn money on their own terms. This flexibility is appealing to many individuals looking to supplement their income or transition to full-time self-employment.

Overall, the combination of AI, blockchain, VR, AR, and the gig economy is creating a wealth of opportunities for individuals looking to make $1000 a month from home in 2024. By staying informed about these emerging technologies and leveraging them to their advantage, individuals can take control of their financial futures and build successful home-based income streams.

Predictions for the Future of Remote Work

As we look ahead to the future of remote work, it is clear that the landscape is rapidly evolving. With advancements in technology and a growing acceptance of remote work arrangements, the possibilities for earning a home-based income are greater than ever before. In this chapter, we will explore some predictions for the future of remote work and how you can capitalize on these trends to make $1000 a month from the comfort of your own home.

One prediction for the future of remote work is the continued rise of flexible work arrangements. As more companies embrace remote work as a viable option for their employees, the traditional 9-to-5 office job may become a thing of the past. This shift towards flexibility opens up new opportunities for individuals to create their own schedules and work from anywhere in the world, making it easier than ever to earn a home-based income.

Another prediction for the future of remote work is the increased demand for skilled freelancers and independent contractors. As businesses look to cut costs and streamline their operations, they are turning to freelance professionals to fill specific roles on a project-by-project basis. This trend presents a unique opportunity for individuals with specialized skills to market themselves and secure high-paying remote work opportunities.

Additionally, the rise of the gig economy is expected to continue in the coming years, providing even more avenues for individuals to earn a home-based income. Platforms like Uber, TaskRabbit, and Fiverr have revolutionized the way people work and connect with clients, making it easier than ever to find freelance gigs and side hustles that can supplement your income. By tapping into the gig economy, you can diversify your income streams and increase your earning potential from home.

In conclusion, the future of remote work is bright, with endless possibilities for individuals to earn a home-based income. By staying informed about industry trends and embracing new opportunities for remote work, you can position yourself for success in 2024 and beyond. Whether you are looking to supplement your current income or transition to a full-time remote career, there has never been a better time to explore the world of remote work and unlock your earning potential from the comfort of your own home.

Adapting to Changes and Staying Ahead in the Home-Based Income Game

In the fast-paced world of home-based income, it's crucial to adapt to changes and stay ahead of the game in order to succeed. As technology and market trends continue to evolve, it's important for adults looking to make $1000 a month from home in 2024 to stay informed and constantly update their skills and strategies. By being proactive and staying ahead of the curve, you can ensure that your home-based income remains steady and profitable.

One key way to adapt to changes and stay ahead in the home-based income game is to stay informed about industry trends and new opportunities. With the rise of remote work and the gig economy, there are more ways than ever to make money from home in 2024. By staying up-to-date on the latest trends and opportunities, you can position yourself to take advantage of new income streams and stay ahead of the competition.

Another important aspect of adapting to changes in the home-based income game is to continuously update your skills and knowledge. As technology evolves and market demands shift, it's important to stay relevant and competitive by learning new skills and staying current with industry best practices. Whether it's taking online courses, attending workshops, or seeking out mentorship opportunities, investing in your professional development is essential to staying ahead in the home-based income game.

Networking is also a crucial component of adapting to changes and staying ahead in the home-based income game. By connecting with other professionals in your niche, you can stay informed about industry developments, exchange ideas, and potentially collaborate on new projects. Building a strong network of like-minded individuals can provide you with valuable resources and support as you navigate the ever-changing landscape of home-based income.

In conclusion, adapting to changes and staying ahead in the home-based income game requires a proactive and strategic approach. By staying informed about industry trends, updating your skills and knowledge, and networking with other professionals, you can position yourself for success in making $1000 a month from home in 2024. By embracing change and staying ahead of the curve, you can ensure that your home-based income remains profitable and sustainable in the years to come.

Chapter 9: Conclusion: Achieving Financial Freedom through Home-Based Income

Reflecting on Your Home-Based Income Journey

Reflecting on your home-based income journey can offer valuable insights into your progress and growth as you navigate the world of remote side hustles. As you look back on where you started and where you are now, take the time to appreciate how far you have come and the effort you have put into building your income streams from home.

One key aspect of reflecting on your home-based income journey is tracking your successes and failures. By keeping a record of your earnings, expenses, and the strategies you have used to generate income, you can identify what has worked well for you and what areas may need improvement. This data can help you make informed decisions about where to focus your time and energy moving forward.

Another important aspect of reflecting on your home-based income journey is setting goals for the future. By looking back on what you have achieved so far, you can create realistic and achievable goals for the coming months and years. Whether you aim to increase your monthly income, diversify your income streams, or improve your work-life balance, setting clear goals can help keep you motivated and on track.

Reflecting on your home-based income journey also provides an opportunity to celebrate your successes. Take the time to acknowledge and appreciate the milestones you have reached, no matter how small they may seem. Celebrating your achievements can boost your confidence, reinforce your commitment to your goals, and inspire you to continue pushing forward in your home-based income endeavours.

In conclusion, reflecting on your home-based income journey is a valuable practice that can help you assess your progress, set goals, and celebrate your successes. By taking the time to look back on where you started and where you are now, you can gain valuable insights into your growth and development as a remote side hustler. Use this reflection as a tool to guide your future decisions and inspire you to continue pursuing your financial goals from the comfort of your own home.

Celebrating Your Successes and Learnings

As you embark on your journey to make $1000 a month from home in 2024, it's important to take a moment to celebrate your successes along the way. Whether you've just landed your first client or reached a new milestone in your earnings, it's essential to acknowledge and appreciate your hard work and dedication. Celebrating your successes can help boost your morale and motivation, making it easier to stay focused and continue working towards your financial goals.

However, it's also crucial to take the time to reflect on your learnings and areas for improvement. Every setback or mistake is an opportunity to learn and grow, so don't be discouraged by them. Instead, use them as stepping stones to better yourself and your business. By identifying what went wrong and how you can do better next time, you can continue to evolve and become more successful in your home-based income endeavours.

One way to celebrate your successes and learnings is to keep a journal or log of your achievements and setbacks. This can help you track your progress over time and provide valuable insights into your strengths and areas for improvement. By regularly reviewing your journal, you can stay motivated and focused on your goals, while also gaining a deeper understanding of your business and how to make it thrive.

Another way to celebrate your successes and learnings is to share them with others. Whether it's with a close friend, family member, or mentor, talking about your achievements and setbacks can be incredibly rewarding. Not only can it help you gain valuable feedback and advice, but it can also provide a sense of accountability and support as you continue on your journey to making $1000 a month from home in 2024.

In conclusion, celebrating your successes and learnings is an important part of the journey to creating a successful home-based income. By taking the time to acknowledge your achievements and reflect on your setbacks, you can stay motivated, focused, and continuously improve your business. So, take a moment to celebrate how far you've come, and use your learnings to propel yourself even further towards your financial goals.

Taking Action towards Your $1000 a Month Goal in 2024

Now that you have set your goal of making $1000 a month from home in 2024, it's time to take action and start working towards achieving it. In this subchapter, we will discuss some practical steps you can take to kickstart your journey towards financial success.

The first step towards reaching your $1000 a month goal is to assess your skills and interests. What are you good at? What do you enjoy doing? By identifying your strengths and passions, you can choose a side hustle that aligns with your talents and interests, making it more likely for you to succeed.

Once you have identified your strengths and interests, it's time to start researching potential opportunities for making money from home. This could include freelance writing, virtual assisting, online tutoring, or selling handmade crafts on platforms like Etsy. Take the time to explore different options and determine which one is the best fit for you.

After selecting a side hustle that resonates with you, it's crucial to create a detailed plan of action. Set specific, measurable goals for yourself, such as how many hours you will dedicate to your side hustle each week and how much money you aim to make per month. By outlining your goals and creating a roadmap for achieving them, you will be more likely to stay focused and motivated.

In addition to creating a plan, it's essential to stay organized and disciplined in your approach to reaching your $1000 a month goal. Set up a dedicated workspace in your home, establish a routine that allows for consistent work on your side hustle, and track your progress towards your financial target. By staying organized and disciplined, you will set yourself up for success in achieving your goal of making $1000 a month from home in 2024.

In conclusion, reaching your $1000 a month goal in 2024 is entirely possible with the right mindset, skills, and dedication. By assessing your strengths, researching opportunities, creating a plan of action, and staying organized and disciplined, you can turn your dream of financial success into a reality. Take action today and start working towards achieving your goal – the possibilities are endless when it comes to making money from home in 2024.

www.ingramcontent.com/pod-product-compliance
Lightning Source LLC
Chambersburg PA
CBHW070127230526
45472CB00004B/1455